Marketing Quarterly series, William J. Winston, Editor:

*the Group Practice: Practical Methods for the Health
itioner*

for Mental Health Services

Long-Term and Senior Care Services

s in Hospital Marketing

Ambulatory Care Services

Strategies for Human and Social Service Agencies

ABOUT THE EDITOR

Winston is Dean of the School of Health Services
, Golden Gate University, San Francisco and Manag-
e of the Professional Services Marketing Group, a
consulting firm in San Francisco.

Mark
Ambulatory

The *Health*

- *Marketing
  Care Pra*
- *Marketing*
- *Marketing*
- *Innovatio*
- *Marketing*
- *Marketing*

William
Managemer
ing Associa
health mark